# PUSHIN'
# NINETY

## Virginia Bathurst Beck

ISBN: 978-1-4907-2034-0 (sc)
ISBN: 978-1-4907-2035-7 (e)

*Trafford rev. 04/16/2014*

 www.trafford.com
North America & international
toll-free: 1 888 232 4444 (USA & Canada)
fax: 812 355 4082

# DEDICATION

**FAVORITE TEACHERS AND
WHAT I LEARNED FROM THEM**

**Mr. Fowler—(Jr. High Teacher)**
Stealing apples on the way home from
school is *really stealing.*

**Miss Hoyt—(Sr. High Principle)**
The only ones who never fail are those who never try.

**FAMILY TEACHERS**

**Roland J. Bathurst—(My Dad) (This was his first job.)**
He taught me how to laugh.

**Cheryl Adkins—(My Daughter)**
She taught in South Korea and said she loved it.
So we visited her there

**Richard Bathurst (My Nephew)**
He taught me that Teacher Coaches
shouldn't punch the umpire.

**Gary Bathurst (My Nephew)**
He is one who carries on the family's singing tradition.

# PROLOGUE

I've had such a wonderful life I just want to share it with everyone. That's one of the reasons I'm writing these books now. I wrote my first column when I was eighty years old. I wrote my first book at 88, "LIFE BEGINS AT EIGHTY" using those columns. That book was successful, so I decided to write a second one: "PUSHIN' NINETY". I passed that landmark 90 year birthday, this year March 27, 2013. I have plans to write six more books and my publisher, The Trafford Publishing Company, has plans to publish my first two as Audio Books. Hope I'm still around to accomplish all this!

I have written something all my life, but just for fun, not profit. I have written for school papers, publicity for clubs, skits for school assemblies, and funny poetry for the amusement of myself or my friends. I have lived in Blair for 60 years where I belonged to Community Theatre and wrote publicity for them. I also sang, danced and acted in their productions.

The first money that I earned for my writing was when I was eighty and started writing a column for the Zapata News in Zapata, Texas. That was our winter home at the time. It was followed by a column in The Star Newspaper in Port St. Joe, Florida, where we wintered next. Then I wrote for the Enterprise Newspaper in our Old Hometown of Bla1r, Nebraska. I wrote those columns for eight years.

Then I thought, if I didn't get started soon I would never get a book published, so I decided to write a book from the columns I had written. As I didn't start writing columns until I was eighty that influenced the title of my first book. Here both are:

First book
**"LIFE BEGINS AT EIGHTY"**

Second Book
**"PUSHIN' NINETY"**

## End of The Trail

*Virginia Bathurst Beck*

*This is the heading for the first column I wrote. It was for the Star Newspaper in Port St. Joe, Florida. I was 81 years old at the time. I was ecstatic to say the least. I didn't feel or look 81 but I was.*

*Two years later I started a second column in Blair Nebraska where we had lived for 50 years. I knew most everyone who lived there and I loved the feed back I got from them. This heading was used by the Pilot Tribune Newspaper.*

## Back to the Border

*Two years after that I started "BACK TO THE BORDER" for the Zapata News in Zapata. Texas. After we retired this was our winter home. We lived there winters for 18 years then moved to Florida where our son, Dan lived.*

# CHAPTER ONE

# BEGINNING AGAIN

The above picture is of my husband and I taken when we had been married about 5 years. It was taken at an old time dance hall that we ran at that time in Sioux City, Iowa. We were having a square dance party, so we dressed up for it.

# SIXTY FIFTH ANNIVERSARY

## 65 YEARS—WOW

Celebrating our 65th Wedding Anniversary made me stop and take notice. Notice of what? Well, notice of all the changes that have taken place in our lives since we were married. There were big changes that have altered the world. I'll tell you how those have affected us and altered our lives.

## NO CAR—AND BROKE

When we were married we didn't even own a car and had only fifty dollars between us. I lost those fifty dollars when my purse was either lost or stolen. We ended up borrowing a car and the money to go on a 'honeymoon', but on a 'honeymoon' we went. Our first child was born just nine months later . . .

## COLLEGE GRADUATION

My husband Danny's brother Art was attending Barber College on the "G. I. Bill". Danny figured that 'what Art could do, he could do', so he enrolled as well. He felt he had at least earned that much with the 38 months he had served "in active duty" during WWII. I worked part time until he graduated. Then he and Art became Barbers like their father. Those of you who don't know what the G I. Bill was, it was a bill passed to ensured that all who served honorably in the war would get their college tuition paid for by the government.

The brothers worked several years at different shops, then bought their own shop in Blair, Nebraska. Danny worked 23 years in the Blair Shop then sold out to Art and started a construction company. He always wanted to be an Architect and I guess that he figured that would be the next best thing. He built 10 houses before we retired in 1986. I say we retired because I had worked 20 years for Northwestern Bell Telephone Company by that time . . . .

## THE CHANGES WE'VE SEEN

We no longer take our trips on a Greyhound Bus, we drive or fly. The planes are cheaper and faster. Yes! We now have a car. We have 5 vehicles including the antiques and a Motor Home.

We don't write our correspondence by paper and pen, or typewriter and send it by slow mail. We send it by E-mail or Fax.

We no longer sweep our floors, we vacuum them.

We no longer need to go to the library to look something up. We look it up on Internet.

We no longer need to cook supper if we are tired. There are numerous places that we can get take-out for a good "home-like meal". It usually is better than I cook anymore anyway.

There are lots of places that we can buy a tape of our favorite movie and watch it at home. We needn't go out to a Movie Theatre if we don't want to.

## POEM

When we were first married, I wrote a poem especially for Danny. The other day I asked him "whatever happened to that poem that I wrote for you years ago?". He took it out of his billfold. It was all tattered and faded but it was still there. He had carried it for 65 years.

Here it is:

### SALUTE TO A CONDEMNED MAN

AT FIRST SIGHT HE WAS NOTHING—
A SHORT STOCKY CHAP
A SLIGHT STOOP TO HIS SHOULDERS
AND A RED CHECKERED CAP.

HIS FEATURES WERE COMMON
HIS SPEECH A BIT CRUDE
HIS MANNER ON OCCASION
WAS INCLINED TO BE RUDE.

*NO HE HADN'T MUCH CULTURE*
*NOT AS SMOOTH AS THEY COME*
*BUT I FOUND HE WAS ALL*
*THAT I'D WANT AND THEN SOME.*

*HIS ARMS OFFERED A REFUGE*
*FROM THE CRUEL WORLD'S STING*
*WHEN I LOOKED IN HIS EYES*
*I FORGOT EVERYTHING.*

*HIS WORDS THO' UNPOLISHED*
*SET MY HEART IN COMMOTION*
*AS HE HUMBLY PLEDGED*
*HIS UNDYING DEVOTION*

*I KNOW HE WAS SENT*
*FROM HEAVEN ABOVE*
*THIS BOY THAT I CHERISH*
*THIS BOY THAT I LOVE.*

# I CAN'T SING BUT I CAN DANCE

## MY HUSBAND DANCED WITH ME

Second to my love of writing is my love of dancing. When we were first married, my husband danced with me. W-E-L-L,

'He danced at it'. I didn't care how well he danced, I just loved to dance.

I don't know how it came about, but when we had been married about five years, we ran a dance hall for old-time—dancing, mainly 'Square Dancing". Since money was involved, my husband did learn to 'Square Dance." My brother, Raymond had a band in which he played the banjo. His band played for the dances.

## WE HAD A BLAST

As I recall, we loved running it. A good crowd always came, mainly older people. We had to laugh at them coming into the hall. There were quite a few stairs to climb and most of them struggled up. Once they were in, you should have seen them 'two stepping' or 'square dancing' around the hall. Not a limp among them.

## MASQUERADE

Once we had a masquerade ball. Every one of us dressed up for it. My brother, Ray dressed like a Chinaman, my mother-in-law, Effie dressed like an Indian and set in the middle of the floor smoking a pipe. Danny and I dressed in old time costumes as shown on the Chapter One heading. I don't remember how the others dressed.

## LATER

When we retired and moved to our winter home to Zapata, Texas, we had friends that talked us into going square dancing with them. That's the last time that I remember my husband dancing with me. After that I changed to "line dancing". I could do that without him.

## FOND MEMORIES

I line danced at "Falcon Lake West" where we lived, "The Lake Front RV Park", "The Four Seasons RV Park" and "The Legion Hall". I remember those times with the fondest of memories. We now spend winters in Florida where I have to drive 40 miles to line dance. Needless to say, with gas what it costs, I don/t go often.

## I GUESS MY DANCING DAYS ARE OVER!

## JOKE OF THE WEEK

You know you are getting old when everything either dries up or leaks.

# 1940's—ENTERTAINMENT

## NO TV, CDS, OR COMPUTER'S

WOW, you say. What did you kids do for entertainment? Well, you know what they say, you don't miss what you haven't had.

What we did have were phonograph records (old 78s) that we just listened to or got together and danced to. I had an old record of Sophie Tucker. I wish I had that record now. We had radios where we listened to the music, or the weekly 'Soap Operas' or shows like "The Shadow Knows" or comedians like Mutt and Jeff, Amos and Andy or Wheeler and Woolsy.

We had roller rinks that we visited weekly. I saved the 15 cents lunch money Dad gave me and added it to the money I earned so I could go each week. In the winter my friend Ethel and I went ice skating. That was free but it was cold.

I've saved the best 'til last===THE MOVIES. Mom was hooked on them as much as we kids were. She would wait until a really slow night at the theatre and call them. She said she would come with all her kids if they would let us in for half price. She knew they would. The ticket girl checked with the manager and he said YES!

Those movies were what was called "Serial Movies". The ones that I remember most were set in jungles with the good guys running from the bad guys. They would be running across a swinging bridge. The bridge would break and they would fall toward the water and "SNAP". The picture would end and be continued until next week. Next week the good guy would be saved someway and the picture would continue until the next "SNAP". THAT SURE HAD YOU COMING BACK!

## VAUDEVILLES

Sioux City had a theatre called the Orpheum. We kids would be there as soon as the theatre opened on Sunday and run between the three floors, sitting on the plush sofas and looking at the artwork on the walls. When the movie started we would find our way to a front seat and watch the movie. They would show the movie three times with vaudeville shows between. We would stay until the end of the vaudeville shows seeing them twice. Oh boy, they were great shows.

Some of the shows we saw were the comedy teams "Wheeler and Woolsey" and "Laurel and Hardy. We saw the musicians "The Spike Jones Band", Banjo player "Eddy Peabody" and the hefty singer "Martha Ray. And we saw them in person. They were not on T.V. or tapes.

I think that what we had available for entertainment was just as important as T. V. or computers. I think that the kids of today are missing more than we were.

## JOKE OF THE WEEK

Question: When was beef the highest?

Answer: When the cow jumped over the moon.

# I LOVE TO IRON

## MY DAUGHTER DOESN'T

YES! I really do. It is a means of irritation to my daughter. She feels that if the modern materials are dried in a dryer and hung up or folded right away, ironing them is unnecessary. *I don't agree.*

## WHAT I IRONED

I sorted the damp dry clothes out after they are washed. There are two piles, the ones that don't need ironing, and those that I feel an iron would help. I would end up ironing my T-shirts on the reverse side, my husband's shirts, of course, and my slacks to put a better crease in them. However, I wouldn't iron my husband's under shorts as his mother did.

## WHILE WATCHING RERUNS

I save my ironing until reruns of "Matlock", "Murder She Wrote" or "Mash" are on and iron and watch T.V. That's fun for me and its killing two birds with one stone.

I suppose ironing is a holdover from the "good old days". If it is, it's the only part of washing that I would keep.

## DREADED TASK

Washing clothes was one of the most dreaded tasks in keeping house, and it usually took all day.

Just let me give you a rundown from the top. First of all, we didn't have detergent that broke the water and foamed. My mother in law made her own soap with lie and lard. We had to boil the water first with lie to break it before the soap would make suds.

## FIRST WASHING MACHINE

Wash boards and the creek were a little before my time, but, I remember the first washing machine we had. It wasn't electric and I was the one delegated to move the lever back and forth to agitate the clothes.

We run the clothes through a wringer into a tub of rinse water then through the ringer again to get as much water out of them as possible before hanging them outside on the line. They were hung out both in the summer and in the winter. Do you know that clothes will freeze dry? If you live in the South, I don't imagine you have found that out. We brought the overalls and coveralls in the house frozen and stood them up to see how long they would keep their shape before they melted to the floor.

## SPRINKLING THE CLOTHES

We then sprinkled the clothes with water and rolled them up and stuffed them into a basket to be ironed later. I couldn't figure out why we used this process to put more wrinkles in them, and then ironed the wrinkles back out. Now, if I feel something needs to be ironed, I spray them with light spray starch and then iron them. Washing and ironing was one of the things that added to making a housewife's job a fulltime job then.

## JOKE OF THE DAY

While loving your enemy, treat your friends a little better.

# BREAD PUDDING & SUNDAY FUNNIES

## MY FRIEND ETHEL

During my high school years I had a good school chum. She wasn't my only buddy, but she was my favorite. That was because of her mother's 'bread pudding' and the 'Sunday Funnies.'

Ethel and I had a lot in common. We were both pretty good in school, we both liked music and we both liked to skate: ice skate and roller skate and we both came from poor families. We had some of the same classes so we would meet after school, the nights I didn't have to work at a factory, and we'd do our homework together.

## BREAD PUDDING

Those were not the only reason I hung out with her. A couple of times a month I slept over at her house. Her mother was a great cook and baked great bread. It wasn't the bread alone that I especially liked, but on Saturday Night for supper she used up the bread that was left over through the week, and made bread pudding with it. To say it was good pudding was an under statement. IT WAS GREAT! It was so good that it was the only thing they had for Saturday Night Supper!

They usually had many guests besides me and we ate and ate and ate. I wish that I had that recipe now' but I think it was the homemade bread that made it so good and I have never learned to make good home made bread.

## SUNDAY FUNNIES

The second reason that I loved to stay over with Ethel was that we would get up early Sunday Morning to grab the paper before anyone else could get it. It wasn't to see what the latest news was but just to read the "Sunday Funnies". It was a great treat for us to see the saga of "Blondie and Dagwood". I believe that "Dennis the Menace" and his latest adventure was there too. I know that "Moon Mullins", "The Katz and Jammer

Kids" and "Dick Tracy" were there to read. I don't remember any more of the old funnies, but my youth was a long time ago to remember?

## I GOT AWAY FROM THE FUNNIES

When I 'grew up' I had gotten away from reading the funnies. I hadn't read them for years. I was too busy with "more important things", but my husband, Dan, always read them. I just thought of them as one of his idiosyncrasies. Then one day I saw him looking at the paper and laughing hilariously. He looked up and said *"this is so funny"*. I thought of Ethel and I with the funnies spread out on her living room rug reading the funnies and laughing our heads off.

He said "you gotta read this." So I went over and looked at what he was reading. It was 'Blondie and Dagwood'. Pretty soon I was laughing as loud as he was.

## NOT JUST FOR KIDS

Suddenly I realized that funnies were not *'things'* just for kids. They are for adults too. They are for anyone who has a funny bone to be tickled. You'd realize that for a little while you could forget all the bad news you read in the paper. Soon you'd realize that *"reading the funnies was one of the most important things you could do"*!

## JOKE OF THE WEEK

People who think they know it all are a nuisance to those of us who really do.

# CHAPTER TWO

# HAPPY HOLIDAYS

When all our kids were home we made the most of the holidays. Thanksgiving and Christmas. Danny's mother, Effie and step father Charley came, My parents and at least part of the rest of my family came too. We always had a large crowd. One Christmas we had all of both of the families to dinner. There was 30 people in our recreation room . . . . and not one fight. Ha, ha. Art's family, Danny's brother, would take turns hosting the dinners.

**THOSE WERE THE DAYS!**

# VALENTINE DAY

## OFF WITH YOUR HEAD

There are many stories as to how Valentine's Day was started. From Roman History comes the story that two St. Valentines were martyred on February 14th by being beheaded. However Roman Scholars have had great difficulty in finding facts among Roman Valentine Legends to back up that theory.

## BIRDS PAIR OFF

Another story is that the custom of exchanging Valentines on February 14 can be traced to the English Poet, Geoffrey Chaucer. He mentioned that birds began to pair off on that date. I'd rather believe that story as a beginning of Valentine's Day than that two St. Valentines had been beheaded on February 14.

## STARTED IN 1415

According to my sources, Charles, Duke of New Orleans, sent the first Valentine Card in 1415 to his wife. He was imprisoned in the Tower of London at that time.

## BRITIAN

In spite of these sad starts, Valentines Day is celebrated around the world. In Europe it is celebrated in many ways. British children sing special Valentine songs, and receive special gifts. Nearly 60% of all Valentine Cards are purchased in the 6 days prior to the observance, making Valentine's Day a procrastinator's delight.

## STATISTICS

There are 120 single men who are in their 20s for every 100 single women who are of the same age.

There are 33 single men age 65 or older for every 100 single women of the same age. *Where did all the men go ladies?*

Sources: The Aarp Newsletter and The World
Book Encyclopedia.

## JOKE OF THE YEAR

When my husband was courting me he was a prompt suitor with his Valentine Card and his candy. Now he still promptly gives me my card and candy but it is on the day after Valentine's Day. THE CARDS AND CANDY GO ON SALE ON THAT DAY!

# NEW YEAR'S RESOLUTIONS

## NOT YET

I've so far been too busy to write my resolutions for the year. That's my excuse. It's not that I don't recognize my need to change and to pin my intentions to do so down by making my usual resolutions. It's just that I'm tired of making a long list of resolutions for myself and not keeping most of them.

## WEIGHT LOSS

One resolution that I won't need to make this year is to lose weight. That has been on my list for 20 years and I've never kept it. Finally I did. It took the urging of a doctor at the Mayo Clinic where I went to get a check up. I said "urging", but that is just a nice way of saying "chewing out". He asked me why I was trying to kill myself. My blood pressure had gone up, I had an irregular heart beat, I had lost part of my kidney function, and my feet were killing me!!! He called me "obese". That was the first time I was called that by anyone! Believe me! I left his office in a huff, vowing never to come back!

## THE TRUTH HURTS

When my anger wore off, I could see that everything he told me was true. So why was I mad? I was mad because as they say, "the truth hurts". So I slowly lost weight by eating less, walked, and exercised as the doctor had advised. That was in February and by the next December I was down to the goal the doctor had set for me. I could not have done it without the help of the TOPS CLUB (TAKE OFF POUNDS SENSIBLY). At that time I belonged to the club in Zapata, TX. Now I weigh-in at a club in Panama City, FL in the winter and a club in Blair, N.E. in the summer. If I make a resolution this year it will be to eat sensibly, exercise and keep that weight off.

## POLITICAL RESOLUTIONS

This coming year I think it would be fun to make resolutions for someone else. After much thought I have decided to make resolutions for a group who really needs it—CONGRESS.

### ****HERE GOES****

1. I will not tell a lie.
2. I will not resort to character assassination to win an elections.
3. I will put more emphasis on helping education.
4. I will work for the good of the little guy I represent not for big business.
5. I will put up a sign (No Lobbyists Allowed in Congress).
6. I will do all I can to follow the lead of other countries in lowering medical costs.
7. I will keep all my election promises.
8. I will do all I can to pull our boys out of the useless wars and bring our soldiers home to protect our AMERICAN BORDERS.

# OVER THE MEADOW AND THROUGH THE WOODS

## TO GRADMOTHERS HOUSE WE GO

Well Christmas is almost here, but I only have fond memories of my grandmother. She has been gone a long time. Even my parents are long gone. However the love of Christmas they instilled in me still lingers. I love the Christmas Carols that we sing at home and at church. I love the gift cards we get, and I love going through the stores and buying cards and gifts for others. I love the decorations on houses and the window displays in businesses. Especially I love the smiles on faces and the joy everyone is getting out of the season. When I was a kid and lived up North, I loved the snow we usually had at Christmas Time.

## THOSE LESS FORTUNATE

I love the way that people turn out to help those less fortunate than us, like the way the Marine Corp collects and repairs Toys For Tots", the way groups provide baskets for the needy and the way other groups cook dinner for the hungry. I volunteered to help serve the dinners and was surprised at the gratitude of those we served.

## NEIGHBOR HOOD GET TOGETHER

I have very fond memories of the Christmas Dinners that we used to share with our friends and neighbors when we lived in Zapata, Texas. We would all take turns making the turkey and dressing and the others would bring the pies and other trimmings. I don't know if I've had such good eating since then. Most of those people have moved back 'Up North' permanently or passed away. There are a few still living that we keep in touch with.

## HOME IN BLAIR

Our family always celebrated big at Christmas in our hometown of Blair, Nebraska. My mother in law, my brother in law and his wife, and my family always took part in the dinner taking turns serving at their house. The hostess always cooked the meat, usually goose or duck, and the rest brought a favorite dish to add to the meal. One year we were brave enough to serve all of both sides of our families. Dan and I served over 30 people that year.

## LARGEST DINNER

The largest Christmas Dinner we have ever been to was a get together we attended at the R. V. Park where my daughter lived in New Braunfels, Texas. There were nearly 100 people who attended. It was impossible to sample all the dishes, but we tried.

## CHRISTMAS IS INTERNATIONAL

The celebration of Christmas Day is an International Event. It's not just a religious holiday, it's a tradition. No matter what Church Affiliation you have or even if you have none, you can celebrate the Christmas Holiday. You can send a card to those whom you know but do not contact often to let them know you care. You can bask in all the camaraderie that surrounds the holiday and feel much better for it. If we had no Christmas something really good would be missing from our lives.

# I'VE WRITTEN A 'NOT SO GOOD' CHRISTMAS POEM ABOUT NORTH AND SOUTH CHRISTMASES THAT I CAN'T RESIST WRITING ABOUT.

## FLORIDA VS NEBRASKA

Our Florida Xmas is different than most
'Cause not every state is blessed with a coast.

Instead of black ice and blowing snow
We have the whitest of sand, and gentle winds blow.

Instead of stripped trees, when no sap lets them freeze
Florida still has palm trees that sway in the breeze.

The 'North' waits 'til summer to have their floats
But our Xmas Parades have decorated BOATS.

BUT

We both have the spirit of "GOODWILL TOWARD MEN"
So think of us kindly—we'll see you again.

# HOLLOWEEN

## NO TRICK OR TREAT

They don't have trick or treat where we spend our winters now.

When we first came down here, I thought, YUK! How can you celebrate Halloween without "Trick or Treat" *as it turned out you can.*

## EVERY ONE'S PARTY

Our main street business district here in Port St. Joe, Florida is only about 4 blocks long. The city fathers block off all the downtown area and have a party to which the entire town is invited, and a good part of the residents come. All the businesses close and serve drinks and treats outside of their stores. Adults and children alike dress up for the affair. Many people also bring treats to give out.

They hold races, games, costume contests, bob for the apple and have other entertainment. You get to see all the costumes in town, not just those who come to your door at home. It's an extraordinary thing to see and enjoy.

## TRICKIN'

We have always loved Halloween, and made the most of it in Blair when our children were young. We made popcorn ball, fudge, candied apples to give to the kids who came to our door, and our kids brought their fair share of treats home from "Trickin'". We always went through the candy the kids brought home before we let them eat it. We never did find anything wrong with their treats but, needless to say, the sacks were less heavy when they got them back. My husband liked the popcorn balls.

We like both ways of celebrating Halloween. We've had a good time both ways. I believe I do like the idea of the party, because the business people get a chance to participate and the entire town is involved.

Halloween is the children's time to dress up like they want to be. They can be ugly, scary, funny or beautiful. There are no rules as to how you should dress for the occasion.

I have always loved Halloween poems. Here is one my father recited to me when I was a child:

### LITTLE ORPHAN ANNIE

Little Orphan Annie has come to our house to stay.
To wash the pans and kettles up and brush the crumbs away
Shoo the chickens off the porch and wash the floor and sweep
And set the fire and make the bread—earn her board and keep

When we've finished with supper and the dishes all are done
We all gather round the fire and has the mostest fun
Talking about the witches that gather all about
*"And the Goblins that'll get cha if ya' don't watch out"*.

Once there was a little girl who wouldn't say her prayers
And when she went to bed at night—a way upstairs,
Her daddy heard her holler and her momma heard her ball.
And when they turned the covers down, she wasn't there at all.

Just about midnight when the blaze is blue,
And the windmill stutters and the wind goes "W H O O O"
You'd better mind your teachers and your parent fond and dear
And cherish those who love you and dry the orphan's tears
And help the poor and needy ones who gather all about

*"OR THE GOBLINS'L GET YOU"*
*"IF YOU DON'T*
*WATCH OUT"*

# CHAPTER THREE

# DOGS, RATS, AND SQUIRRELS

My life has always included kids and animals. You can't have one without the other. They go together like Wheeler and Woolsey, Amos and Andy, and Lucy and Desi Arnes. I don't imagine that the young people know who I'm talking about. Well ask your grandparents, they'll tell you that they were old time comedians.

Getting back to animals, in this Chapter I'll tell you about the ones that I was associated with in my lifetime.

# DOGGIE DIAPER

## REMEMBER MILLIE

Millie was the dog I wrote about in my first book. The dog that was in the Omaha dog pound. At the time my son Steve and his wife Jeannie adopted her, she had been medically tested by the pound and determined to be terminal. Her one kidney was infected with cancer, they thought, and she wasn't expected to live very long. Sick dogs cannot be adopted so she was scheduled to be put to sleep.

## GOOD TIMES

However Jeannie, who at that time, was an adoption councilor at the Nebraska Humane Society, came to her rescue. She talked the powers that be at the dog pound into letting her take Millie home until she succumbed. Well that was seven years ago and the Lord hasn't let her succumb yet.

Think of all the good times that she and her owners would have missed if they had let them put the dog to sleep, and I would never have come to know her sweet disposition and loving ways.

Also, Millie would never have known the unconditional love and care of her owners and all their friends and relatives.

## ROMPING

In the seven years of her adoption, she has romped joyously with the other dogs that Jeannie and Steve have adopted. She gets knocked down by the bigger dogs and rolls down the hill landing on her feet and gets up running. Many times she has ran down that same hill wagging her tail, to meet her owners or myself. She really has a mind of her own.

## CLIPPING

When she is being clipped, (she has long hair), she stands still and cooperates until they get to clipping the hair on her face. Then she really puts up a stubborn fight. No one can mess with her face.

## VELCRO

A funny episode happened when they were trying to make her comfortable. It was a little cool outside so they put a makeshift overcoat on her and put Velcro on it to hold it together in the front. Then Steve put her in the living room to wait while he drank his coffee. When he was ready to go outside, he called her several times and she didn't move. Well he finally went over to see what was the matter. He found that she had wiggled around until the Velcro had stuck her to the floor. Leave it to Millie!!!

## HER DIAPER

Jeannie was tired of following her around with a cloth cleaning up the drips when she was in the house, so she had finally bought a Doggie Diaper for her. At first Millie fought to get the diaper off but soon became accustomed to it. They didn't use the diaper often, just when she was in the house alone.

## FINAL TRIP

I wonder what the next chapter will bring in this saga of caring people keeping a little doggie alive. Their efforts are not selfish in their mission. Millie does not even know she is terminal. She has many (MOUNTAINS TO CLIMB AND RIVERS TO CROSS) before she makes her final trip.

———

(Millie has gone to heaven since this column was written.) !WE ALL MISS HER!

# OUR PET SQUIRREL

## UNUSUAL PET

Talk about unusual pets, white rats don't hold a candle to one pet we had. The white rats were popular pets back in the olden days, but who ever heard of a pet squirrel? W-e-l-l, the

Bathurst Family did 'cause we had one.' Ya' wonder how that Happened? >>Read on.>>>>>>

## ENTERS RAYMOND

Our family included my youngest brother, Raymond. He was crazy about animals. He wouldn't hunt or do anything that would put animals at risk. This *'pet squirrel'* business started with Ray and the mistake the squirrel made by hanging around our yard waiting to be fed.

## HE COAXED THE SQUIRREL

Well Ray started coaxing the squirrel to let him get closer and closer as he fed him until soon he was taking food from Ray's hand. Then, what do you know? Soon he was letting Ray pick him up.

## RAINS CAME

One day a storm came with wind and rain. Ray happened to look out the door and saw the squirrel standing in the rain, getting soaked in the downpour, waiting for his dinner. Ray couldn't stand it. He ran out, picked up the squirrel, and brought him in the house. We got him a litter box, trained him to use it, and from then on he stayed in the house with us.

## WE PLAYED WITH HIM

We kids had a ball playing running games with our new pet. I think that he enjoyed all the attention too. Perhaps he was a mixture of breeds like dogs are. I think a dog or a cat slipped into his linage. But that's not the end of the story. Read on>>>>>>>>

## THE SLIDING DOORS

We had an old fashioned house with big, sliding doors between the kitchen and the living room. One day mom saw the squirrel trying to get under the door. She grabbed his tail to pull him out and '*OFF CAME HIS TAIL*"!!!

## HE LEFT

Mom almost feinted and the squirrel looked sick. He ran in circles until he was tired. Then he laid down and went to sleep. When he woke from his nap he seemed OK but he didn't have the joy he had being with us as before. One day he just disappeared and never came back. I guess he was out looking around.

*"HE MISSED HIS TAIL"*.

OH! OH!!!

# UNUSUAL PETS

## WHITE RATS

When I was in grade school I had a white rat for a pet. I kept it in a drawer of my dresser. I left the drawer open so he could go in and out. He must have been "house broken" but I don't remember about that. I do remember him coming out of his dresser drawer to play with me when I came home from school.

I don't remember much else. I wish I did. I wish I could remember what was in my head to have a white rat for a pet. I hate rats of any color now but at that time they were a poplar pet.

## DRINKING DOGS—NOT WATER

I didn't know there was such a thing as a drunken dog until I was talking to a fellow at a church supper. He said every once in a while his dog got exceptionally friendly. He didn't act or look like his usually snappy self and the owner decided to take him to have him checked. The Vet couldn't find anything wrong with the dog so he just told the owner to change the brand of food he fed him. He brought home a new brand of dog food and found the dog in his fuzzy condition again.

He happened to look up and see his neighbor laughing at the dog. "Well, what's so funny?" the man said. "I can't find out what is the matter with him". The neighbor said "well he's just drunk". The owner retorted "Who's crazy enough to give a dog liquor"? "Well I am". said the neighbor.

Why do you do that"? said the dog owner. "Because he likes it." stated the neighbor. *WELL YOU CAN'T ARGUE WITH REASONING LIKE THAT.*

## ANOTHER ALCAHOLIC D0G

A woman told me that she and her husband liked to boat and fish. They would take some beer along to help them relax. They took their German Shepherd dog along too. If they put their beer down on the floor, the dog would tip it over to drink the beer that ran out. You can't blame him. He just wanted to relax too.

## A PARTY DOG

Someone else told me that there was a dog at a *(Keg Party)*. When no one was looking, he would drink out of the drip pan of the keg until he was really inebriated. In the morning the dog looked worse than the people leaving the party.

## JOKE OF THE DAY

How do you keep a dog from barking on Sunday Morning?

Shoot him on Saturday night!!!!!

(I know that's gross.)

But it was a favorite joke of the times.

## CHAPTER FOUR

# TRAVELOGUE

## YUCATAN

After we retired and our kids had all flown the coop we traveled. In the summers we worked for our nephew who owns a carnival and in the winters we spent all the carnival money we made traveling. In all we have visited about ten different countries besides what we traveled in the U.S.A.

After about 11 years we retired from both the carnival and the traveling. The following chapter covers some of the places we visited and the foods that we ate there.

# COMMUNICATION

## LACK THERE OF!

It's no wonder that we have a communication problem in the world with all the different languages that are spoken. However language is not the only barrier to communication. People's background, heritage, and religion further complicate their understanding of each other.

Some words, however, seem to be universal. I think that everyone knows the meaning of the word "macho." I don't think you could express the same meaning with an English word. On the other hand, "hot stuff" means different things to different people. To me it means "salsa" and other Mexican food. To a thief it would mean "stolen goods". To a young guy it means "a cute girl".

Several years ago in Wales we became lost while driving on a diversion (detour). We were directed out in the country, but there our signs ended. We stopped at a pub (bar) for directions. One man who was trying to be very helpful gave us directions in English. However his accent was so heavy that it was all "Greek to us

While on an Australian bus trip, we had a hard time deciphering the brogue of the Outback. Not so in the rest of the country.

Traveling on our own in Europe we had no trouble. When we needed information, we talked to someone of high school age. We had learned that in most European countries, four years of English are required first, then two languages of their choice are studied.

I don't know what the answer to our lack of understanding is, but I think it would help to communicate with our hearts as well as our minds.

## ON ANOTHER TOPIC

At one time we spent our winters in Texas on the Mexican border. That was our introduction to the way different countries handled the "restroom" situation. (I hope this offends no one). When we went to Laredo shopping, they didn't have the toilet tissue placed as we do hung inside the stall. A lady set outside and furnished it to us at 10 cents for two sheets. How is that for a sales pitch? The same happened at the small rest stops on our bus trips into Mexico. The paper, in those instances, was supplied outside the facility by our tour guide. I'm sure the cost was included in the price of the trip.

In the London Airport we paid 25 cents to use their facilities. In Germany's Airport the cost was 35 cents but they sprayed the entire inside between customers.

In other countries:

1. In one the people waiting lined up behind the stalls instead of at the door.
2. In another the children's facilities were in front in the open.
3. In another there was no commode, just a hole in the floor.

## JOKES OF THE WEEK

There is no one as narrow minded as he who does not agree with you. Money doesn't make you happy, but it may quiet your nerves.

# A STATE TO TRAVEL IN

## NEBRASKA HAS IT ALL

If you like to travel as much as I do, you can't miss Nebraska. As the title of the paragraph says, Nebraska has it all: It has rivers, hills, valleys, prairies, corn fields, wheat fields and—It has big towns with Live Theatres, Movie Theatres, restaurants, large hotels, shopping malls. Omaha host's The College World Series of Baseball, and the trials for the Olympic Swimming It has small towns with a homelike atmosphere, small grocery stores and some even with Wal-Mart's.

## RIVERS

One River, the Missouri, flows along its top and the Eastern Borders. The Elkhorn flows through the middle of the state.

Then there's the Platte, the Niobrara, the Republican, the Snake, the Calamus and the Sioux Rivers.

The hills and valleys mainly are along the Niobrara River that they share with South Dakota. That area is a fisherman's paradise. It has the most beautiful scenery in Nebraska.

The traffic is good and the people are friendly.

## NEBRASKA FOOTBALL

The Nebraska Football team makes its home at The University of Nebraska which is located at the State Capital of Lincoln. The team has a great following. They say there is "no fans like the Nebraska fans".

The University of Nebraska has more than a good football team. It had the great Coach Osborne who coached that team to several championships. He is retired now but left a great career of 40 years behind him.

## GLORY DAYS

Nebraska has now transferred to the Big Ten and are doing pretty well, but "pretty well" isn't good enough for the "Nebraska Fans". They figure if the team PLAYS HARD ENOUGH, the coaches COACH WELL ENOUGH and if the fans *YELL LOUD ENOUGH,* Nebraska will soon be back to her *GLORY DAYS*.

## WE CAN'T WAIT!!

# TIME TRAVEL

## WENT SKIING

As an avid reader, I read a book a week. I get large print from the library, not to accommodate my sight, but because a large print is easier to read in bed where I do most of my reading.

I just finished a book that fascinated me. It was about 'Time Travel". You see that this lady geologist was being transferred to a new assignment in the Colorado Rockies. She had a few days before she had to report for work, so she went skiing. That was the good part. The bad part was where she went skiing. It was off the beaten path. The trail she should have taken was clearly marked but she felt liked exploring.—OK!

## TROUBLE ON THE SKI PATH

Needless to say she got lost. To make matters worse a blizzard blew in. She fell, broke a ski, and slid down a mountain. Never fear, as in most romances, just before she froze to death a gorgeous guy arrived, rescued her and took her to his cabin. The only trouble was that he was from another millennium. It seems she was so near death that her emotions transferred her from 2012 clear back to 1942. She knew this when he took her to a Military Camp where he was stationed.

## OLD EQUIPMENT

This camp was furnished with military equipment and old cars from many years before and she caught on to the millennium when her drivers license had the year 1942 on it. This was a license from almost 70 years ago and didn't make sense because she was only 30 years old.

## LOVE COMES SOFTLY

Well, of course, they fell in love but since they were from different millenniums, they had a real problem. Everyone at the camp thought she was a spy except, of course, her lover. After she convinced everyone that she wasn't, they had a good time.

## WENT TO TOWN

They went shopping for clothing and, of course loved the 1942 prices since she didn't have much money. One thing she didn't like was the material that all the clothing was made of. 'Wrinkle Free' wasn't heard of in 1942 so she ended up ironing the clothing she bought. Women seldom wore slacks in 1942 and the only shoes that she could buy that she didn't think looked ridiculous were tennis shoes.

## TEENAGERS

They got caught up with some teenagers that were having their High School Prom. They danced with the band that played: "The Boogie Boogie Bugle Boy of Company B", "To Each His Own", then they cuddle danced to "I Found My Thrill On Blueberry Hill."

## TROUBLE

Well it wasn't all peaches and cream. They ran into some real spies who chased them. After a couple of shootouts, her lover of course, overcame the bad guys. They found out that one of the good guys turned out to be the bad guy. *(So what else is new)?* Finally they got together in her world and lived:

## HAPPILY EVER AFTER

After reading this book I've decided that I wouldn't mind living again in 1942. *(That was my year to swing)* That is if I could go to a dance every night and had a Military Hunk to live and dance with. "Sorry Dan"

BUT THEN YOU NEVER DID LEARN TO DANCE!

# MISSED THE TORNADOES

## PLANNED CAREFULLY

We finally left Florida for Nebraska after we planned and packed and gave away stuff and loaded the car. Our planning consisted of choosing a trip that would miss the tornadoes. Since they had already had tornadoes in Kansas, Oklahoma and Missouri we planned to miss those states. Virginia had also had a tornado so we wanted to miss that state too. The plan we came up with was a route between the tornado states.

## LONG LIST OF TAKE-ALONGS

We had decided to take just one suitcase apiece but we ended up packing four. This would probably be the last time that we came in a car so there were many other things we should take. The list seemed endless. There were fishing poles for the great grand kids, two bird baths for son Steve, two big bags of pecans for everyone, yard goods and material for crafts for me to work with, the cooler full of food, six notebooks full of my columns so I can work on that book I may never finish, folders with copies of my dads recitation and funny songs that I plan to give each relative at Christmas, and a box full of old antique Harley Davidson Bandanas that I want someone to sell for me on internet.

## AWAY WE GO

We gave away all of the perishable foods in our refrigerator to the neighbors, crowded everything in our car and was on our way. We left home at 6:30 A.M. our time which was 5:30 Central Standard Time.

## MISSED THE FIRST ONE

The first day out was great. We were in a good mood and taking off for another adventure. The first nights stop was a little past Montgomery, Alabama. We started the next day at 6:30 and stopped for breakfast about 10:00 O'clock. We had planned to get to Memphis, Tennessee by night fall but we were held up over an hour by road construction. We were tired when we got to Tupelo, Mississippi, so we stayed all night there. When we went to supper we learned that they had just had a tornado in Memphis. If we hadn't have been held up, we would have been there about the time it hit. Since the tornado was over, we decided to go our original route through Memphis. O K!

## MISSED THE SECOND ONE

We stopped in New Albany for breakfast and learned that a bad tornado hit them after the one had hit Memphis. We saw destruction along the hi-way upon leaving the town. There were trees down all over and road signs mutilated. We held our breath the rest of the way home. I guess that helped because no tornados caught up with us.

It was late when we reached Blair, but Steve brought his dog Millie out to welcome us.

## MISSED THE LAST TORNADO

Needless to say we went to bed early. When we got up the next morning and turned the news on, the first thing we heard was that a tornado had just hit Tupelo, Mississippi. Oh Boy! We missed the bullets. I think we'll fly after this and let the pilots watch for tornados. I don't think they'll fly through them.

## JOKE OF THE WEEK

The only sure way of doubling you money is to fold it over and put it back in your pocket.

# CHAPTER FIVE

| Dan Beck | Virginia Beck | Bob Boozer & Charles Adkins | John Adkins | Danny Adkins | Cheryl Adkins |

## I REMEMBER

During my lifetime I have met many wonderful people that I can't forget nor do I want to forget them. In this chapter I want to give you an explanation of how they affected my life and why I don't want to forget them. "THEY HAVE GONE BUT THEY NEVER WILL BE FOGOTTEN BY ME."

# BOB BOOZER

**Bob Boozer and I**

## TEN JOBS

In my lifetime I have had ten different jobs. Working at Northwestern Bell Telephone Company was the best and the last job that I had. I retired from the company after twenty years service. Bob Boozer was a part of that.

## PLAYED BASKETBALL

I'm certain that many of you too remember him. He was a very successful basketball player with the Chicago Bulls. When he ended his basketball career he was hired into management by Northwestern Bell. At that time I worked at the downtown Public Office at twentieth and Douglas. He became our manager.

## DODGE BALL

Bob and I hit it right off. I don't know why. Perhaps it was because he was such a nice person and treated his employees so well. The downtown office was not an easy place to work. The inside Service Representatives would shut off service for non—payment of their bill and the customer would come in and take it out on us in the Public Office. Once I had a chair thrown at me. It missed. I guess that "Dodge Ball" I played in grade school finally paid off.

One day I asked Bob how he handled the irate customers. He said that if they came in yelling at him he just stood up to his full seven foot height and they back off, shut up, and paid their bill. That couldn't work for me because I'm only five foot two inches tall.

## CHOCOLATE LABS

Once I was showing Bob some pictures of the Chocolate Labrador Dogs that we raised. He said that he wouldn't mind having one of those, so I promised him one of the next liter.

When he came to get the dog he brought his wife and little boy with him and they chose a puppy.

## THE PICTURE I NEVER SHOT

I have a charming picture of a little black boy walking across our patio with one puppy in his arms and with three other puppies following him. That picture remains only in my mind because I never shot it. Don't ask me why. I've missed snapping it for a long time.

## SMILING DOGS

The mother of the puppy they chose was named Tricksy. She was a 'smiling dog.' None of the rest of the dogs in that litter were smiling dogs, so I wondered if Bob's was. You didn't know until the dog got older and by that time Bob and I were both transferred elsewhere in the company so I didn't find out until much later.

One day a young couple came to our house to buy one of our dogs. I don't know why but we got around to talking about smiling dogs. The guy said his job was picking up trash in Omaha. He told us their was a smiling dog on his route and it was a Black Lab. When he told us the area he worked in, I recognized it as the area Bob lived in. So maybe Bob did get one after all.

## RETIREMENT

Well finally *all things come to him who waits*. After twenty years it finally came time for my retirement. W0W! I asked if Bob could speak at my retirement party. The powers that be said that by company policy it had already been set up that my immediate manager would speak. Well, if you know me you know that this wouldn't be the last word. So, I asked Bob to speak also, and they couldn't say no to Bob. So it all worked out. I had two great speakers at my retirement party.

## GONE BUT NOT FORGOTTEN

The last I heard of Bob was when he was on the Parole Board at some of the Nebraska Prisons. I know this because my grandson, Danny worked at one as a security guard and got to talk to him occasionally.

Bob died too young. I know that he must still have had places to go and things to do before he was gone. However—:

*HE HAD ALREADY ACCOMPLISHED MUCH SO THAT HE LEFT A LONG LEGACY OF THINGS HE HAD DONE FOR HUMANITY . . .*

# TRIBUTE TO ANDY

## FOND MEMORIES

I had not seen or talked to Andy Sorenson for a number of years. We were then spending our retirement years in Texas. However my fond memories of him and my admiration for his singing talent had not diminished over the years.

## SHOCKED

I was shocked to learn that he had died suddenly at a very young age. I was not surprised to learn of all his successes in his short career as a teacher.

## COMMUNITY THEATRE

I met Andy when he was a young teenager. We were both active in Community Theatre. Once I was cast as "Aunt Polly" and he as "Tom Sawyer" in the play of the same name. He impressed me then with both his responsibility and his talent.

## TROUBLE

I had much trouble learning my part in the play and hung on to my copy of the script as long as I could. On the other hand, Andy learned his part early and helped me with my lines as much as possible. He even covered for me once when I missed my cue during a performance.

My off-key alto didn't "hold a candle" to his magnificent tenor voice. That's how I'll always remember Andy—as this young red haired Tom Sawyer—standing center stage—in his worn shirt and bib overalls—with one strap over his shoulder—and singing his heart out.

## THE HEREAFTER

I'm sure there is more important work planned for him in the hereafter—either singing with the angels or perhaps as directing their Heavenly Chorus.

## FAREWELL AND GOD SPEED ANDY

Andy has been gone from us a long time, but I thought it appropriate to put it in this book now.

# JOHNNY CARSON

## NORFOLK

The closest that I ever came to a "claim of fame" is that we shared a state with Johnny Carson, namely Nebraska. For a time we even shared the same town, Norfolk. My husband's first job after he graduated from college, (Barber College that is) was at Faubel's Barber shop in Norfolk. While Danny was learning to clip hair, Johnny was starting out as a magician. Of course he wasn't yet famous so we had no idea who he was then, or how famous he would eventually become.

## DUSTED OFF SIGN

Later we moved to Blair where Dan and his brother, Art bought a barber shop. What do you know, Johnny followed us there. Well, he didn't actually follow us but he did come to Blair often to visit his grandfather who spent many years in Blair's Crowell Nursing Home, After his grandpa passed away, he only came to Nebraska to visit the rest of his family that lived in Norfolk. It was in the news each time he came. The joke then was that he came to dust off the sign outside of Norfolk that said: "Home Town of Johnny Carson".

## FABULOUS CAREER

Of course we followed his career. I think that is the only time in our lives that we have ever stayed up after 10 P. M. It was to watch "The Tonight Show" with Johnny Carson. A laugh with Johnny before we retired was funny and relaxing.

He was always willing to give new talent a start and give other entertainers a boost up. It was a prime shot to be on his show as there weren't any other ways then to show off your talent as there are today.

## AUCTION

Now and auction is being held. They will be selling many of his entertainment mementos, including his desk and his microphone. They are expecting to make a bundle on the auction and they probably will. That is one auction that I'd like to attend, but I couldn't afford the prices.

I have one up on them though. For years we have had a joke book written by Johnny and illustrated by Whitney Darrow Jr. and published by Doubleday in 1965. It is in the Library of Congress, Catalogue no. 65458. It is a 4 x 5 book of Johnny's jokes titled: "Happiness is a Dry Martini" Here are some of his jokes:

## HAPPINESS IS:

1. Having the finance company burn down with all your records.
2. Your knee length socks stay up all day.
3. The smart aleck who is voted Most Likely To Succeed makes it>>on the FBI's Most Wanted List.
4. Being served with a paternity suit on your 75th birthday.

He is deceased now but not retired. He is up their probably entertaining the angels.

## CHAPTER SIX

# MISCELLANEOUS

These columns didn't fit into any other category, but I had to use them. SO HERE WE GO!

# DRUG COUNTRY

## EXPLANATION

I wrote this article in Texas for my former boss, Bob McVey, who was then owner and Editor of the Zapata News. We lived near Hi-Way 83 which goes south along the Rio Grande River that serves as the border between the U. S. and Mexico. Hi-way 83 was known as "Drug Row" by locals, as it was used as the main route for getting drugs from Mexico to the U. S. The truck I speak of was impounded because it was used to carry contraband to the U. S. When I read Bob's column claiming a conversation with the truck, I couldn't resist the following answer in another article:

## THE ERRANT TRUCK

Bob, I've enjoyed all of your columns, but I was especially intrigued by the one that appeared in the July 16th paper. I'm referring to the recount of your conversation with the *errant truck* that ended up in the 'hoosegow'—sorry, the 'local impound lot'. You said that the truck started talking to you as you passed by. He (the truck) tried to convince you that even though he carried the drug dealers and their load of pot down Hi-way 83 and through every stop sign in Zapata with the cops on their tail and finally ended up in a ditch where they were finally apprehended, it wasn't his fault. It was the drug dealers fault.

Bob assuming permission, I would like to give you a piece of advice that you can pass on to the truck the next time you are in whatever condition you were in when you talked to it before.

### "EXCUSES!"

Dear Mr. Truck:

"As a grandmother that has been around a Zapata block a time or two, I'll tell you as I have told my kids and grand kids; DON'T CRY TO ME THAT SOMEONE GOT YOU INTO TROUBLE. 'You should choose your friends more carefully'—'birds of a feather flock together'—'you are the Captain of your ship (or truck', 'you are the Master of your fate' etc."

### "EXCUSES"

"Just because you were manufactured in a permissive era, doesn't cut *no ice with me*. You were responsible for your own irresponsible actions when you were busted for 'aiding and abetting' drug dealers by hauling their pot. In your own words you appealed to Bob, and I quote: "But it wasn't my fault. I'm innocent. They can't blame me. I'm a good truck but people just keep misusing me."

## "EXCUSES!"

"Poppycock! Excuses! Excuses! Excuses! I've heard all that before! You knew what you were getting into when they loaded that pot. Right then you could have pulled that old dead battery trick that my car pulls now and then. When your partners in crime commanded you to run from the cops, you could have died at every stop sign as my car does for no good reason. No it seems that you enjoyed that 'heck of a ride' down main street when you tried to outrun the cops. You just sped on, ignoring the stop signs and never missing a beat".

## REHABILITATION

"I could go on berating you and telling you all of the tricks that a 'good truck' could have pulled to keep from helping the bad guys but I won't. I believe everybody and everything can be rehabilitated with plenty of tender, loving, care."

"The only help that I can see for you, however, is if a good family adopts you and gives you the reconstruction and the discipline you obviously need. Hey! The next time you talk to Bob, you could mention the idea to him. Maybe he could find some use for a good truck around the newspaper. Then on a bad day, when no one at work was talking to him, you could return the favor by letting him come out and talk to you again!!"

# DOING SOMETHING DIFFERENT

## HURRAH!

We did something different last weekend. In this case something different meant not sitting in front of television with our eyes glued to the screen watching a football being kicked, passed, maneuvered, squashed, turned over, recovered, scrunched, cuddled and coached from one end of the field to the other.

This done by players who smiled, yelled, hugged and played the crowd when their players made a touchdown, but cursed, frowned, grumbled and growled when the other team did.

## LIGHT, ACTION, CAMERA

Whoever writes the script for those football T V shows doesn't have much imagination because the actors, sorry I meant players, make the same moves every show. The only thing that you don't know will happen is WHO WILL WIN THE GAME!!! I could tell you that. It's usually THE OTHER TEAM. Sorry guys. That's just a woman's view of football and you know that doesn't count for much.

The 'something different' we did was not 'storm chasing' but it was 'flood dodging'. Since we are in Nebraska now, we decided to go to Fremont about 20 miles from Blair. Sadly to say, neither of us had watched the news that morning so little did we know that the Fremont area was surrounded by flood waters.

## GOING IN CIRCLES

The first we were aware of floods was when we were stopped at a road block and sent on another road. We weren't familiar with that road so we drove and drove and drove. When we were just about to turn around and go back another road block came up and a man put us on a different road we didn't know and told us to drive until we came to hi-way 64 turn right on hi-way 275 then left on hi-way 30 to Fremont. You know what? WE DID IT!

## GOING HOME

After we had finished our shopping, and eaten lunch, we headed back to Blair with confidence. So we left town on hi-way 30 turned onto 275 and turned on what we thought was 64. —*It wasn't.*

After we had gone a long ways we run into another road block. A maintenance man sent us clear back to Hi-way 275 and told us to turn left to Hi-way 31. then right, then left, then right again. From there we knew OUR WAY HOME.

## WATER, WATER, EVERYWHERE

I never saw so much water in my life. It seems the Elkhorn River had flooded from clear up in Northern Nebraska and it was everywhere covering yards, sheds and bridges.

I think next week-end we'll go back to watching football. It doesn't take gas and WE'RE NEVER LOST.

## JOKE OF THE WEEK

SARCASM: The gulf between the author of sarcastic wit and the person who doesn't get it.

## CHAPTER SEVEN

# KICKIN' THE BUCKET

**I STILL HAVE SOME MORE**

**COLUMNS THAT I WANT**

**YOU TO READ AND I JUST**

**DON'T WANT TO THROW**

**THEM OUT. SO I'LL JUST**

**TOSS THEM IN A BUCKET**

**AND YOUR JOB WILL**

**BE TO 'KICK THE BUCKET'**

**AND SEE WHAT COMES**

**OUT.**

# MY FIRST CAREER

## BEAUTY SCHOOL

When I graduated from High school, I bypassed going to college. My folks didn't have the money to send me but a favorite teacher wanted to put me through school. She had never married and had no children that she needed to educate. I don't know why she had always admired me but she had, and said that if she could help me become a teacher or a lawyer instead of working for a low wage at some restaurant or dime store she would have accomplished something with the money she had saved.

## SHE WENT WITHOUT

I saw the way she dressed at school. She wore the same dress daily and changed it only when we had a school program or she went to church. She saved every penny of her money that she could. I was proud enough that I couldn't spend the money she had gone without to save. I told her NO but THANK YOU! I said that if I wanted to go to college so badly, I would work and save my own money and pay my own way. I have never forgotten that teacher or the good influence she had on my life.

## I WON A COLLEGE SCHOLARSHIP

What do you know? I won a College Scholarship. It wasn't for the college of my dreams; it was a scholarship to attend Beauty College. That was a natural for me as I had always fixed the neighbor's hair without a license.

Before I went to school, I checked out each state to see how many training hours they required to get a license. Utah had the fewest. It took only 1500 training hours there and 2100 in Iowa. So as soon as I had my 1500 hours worked out in Sioux City, I said a tearful good bye to my family, and rode the old Challenger Train to Ogden Utah, took their test and got my license in Utah.

## FINGER WAVES AND ELECTRIC PERMS

I worked a year and a half in that shop. Those were the Days of finger waves and electric permanents. I worked part time and attended Webber College part time. Those were the first college credits that I earned and Beauty Culture was my first real job.

Ogden was "Mormon Country". My landlady was a Mormon, the grocer was Mormon, the teachers were Mormons and my friends were all Mormons. They were the friendliest people I've ever met. They just took me in and made me one of them. I respected their religion and they respected mine.

## THE BISHOPS GARDEN

They all seemed to take care of each other. One thing that I admired most was what was called the 'Bishop's Garden'. The Church owned land that they divided into plots. Those who wished to could use one of those plots to grow their vegetables on. That's where I learned to like gardening.

## SOMETHING ELSE

Something else I did while attending Weber College was to write scripts for the assemblies. My writing teacher assigned me to do this. At first I didn't think myself capable, but with the teacher's faith in me and her encouragement, I was soon organizing shows for the assemblies and loving it. I was not only using college students, but I was "showcasing" all the surrounding talent. We had many outsiders come to see our shows. I think it was then that I decided to become a writer.

Loving the people, the college, and my work, you wonder why I ever left Ogden, Utah. Well—Don't forget my wandering foot. After two years it started itching and so I waved goodbye to all my friends and I was "ON THE ROAD AGAIN".

## SAN FRANCISCO

Next I moved with a friend I had met to San Francisco. I worked as a waitress for Bunny's Waffle Shop which was one of a chain of restaurants located in the area. I was soon promoted to bookkeeper of the restaurant.

San Francisco was an interesting place. There was much to do. I went swimming in the ocean, went horseback riding in Golden Gate Park, and went Christmas Shopping in China Town. Although I didn't drink, my friend, Ethel and I went to every bar on Powel Street, drinking soft drinks and listening to the great live music.

## GO'IN HOME

By that time I was 22 years old and homesick. I was also convinced that I was having a "nervous breakdown." I went home to be consoled by my mother. I had read somewhere that hard physical activity would cure any case of nerves. So I got a job at a dairy washing out their vats. Soon my nervous condition was cured and they had promoted me to Assistant Lab Manager.

## *'LOTSA' JOBS*

I worked in a factory after school while in High School, in a Beauty Parlor, was a Civil Service Secretary at Sac Air Force Base while it was based in Ogden Utah, as a waitress, and a bookkeeper twice, an Assistant Lab Manager an Aria Sales Manager for World Book Encyclopedia, a Telephone sales Representative for a roofing company. *Lotsa' jobs, HUH?* I had at least 12 jobs the 6 years before I was married to Dan Beck and had my 3 children.

## LAST JOB

The last job I had was for NorthWestern Bell Telephone Company. I went to work for them when my daughter was ready for college and worked for them 20 years. Either I was tired of running around the country or Dan was a good influence on me.

## JOKE OF THE DAY

Doctor: "Nobody lives forever."

Patient: "Mind if I try

# FLACK!

## SLEPT ALL NIGHT

I have taken a lot of flack over a lot of things but never more than I took when my first child, a daughter, was born. I opted to do what my pediatrician told me to do. First of all, I trained her to sleep through the night. If she woke up after her nine P.M. feeding, I gave her only water. The doctor told me that water was satisfying to babies but was not habit forming as milk was. If they got milk at night they kept waking up for it.

## LYING ON HER STOMACH

If I remember right, she learned to sleep all night when she was 3 or 4 weeks old. It was better for the baby and certainly better for us. He told us to let her sleep on her stomach without a pillow to prevent her head from becoming flat in the back. According to him a baby could turn it's head from side to side and without a pillow, there was no chance of suffocating. I know that doctors think differently now but I never had any trouble. He also told me to put her on a four hour schedule for her meals and always to hold her for her bottle feeding. Since I couldn't nurse her that was as close as I could get to a natural feeding. I never laid her down with a bottle in her mouth.

## COMES THE FLACK

Oh! Boy! Did I ever hear it from my mother, my mother-in—law, the next door neighbor, my friends and on and on. . . . . They all told me that they didn't raise their children that way, but they all had a different way that they thought was better. Since I couldn't choose from them which way to raise her, I decided to stick with what the pediatrician said I should do. It seemed to be working well and everyone finally grudgingly accepted my way.

## "I DID IT MY WAY"

Whenever I mentioned that she didn't get any sugar treats, you would think that she was being abused. "You mean she doesn't get a piece of candy or a cookie with her milk. Think what she is missing?" I answered that as far as I can see, she is missing bad teeth and unhealthy fat deposits at a young age. I said that I agree. Candy is delicious. Cookies are delicious. I said that someday my daughter would have sugar, but I'd like to postpone it as long as possible. Once she's tried sugar that's it! It's a habit! A habit that rots our teeth, makes us put on weight, and raises havoc with our blood chemistry. Once we've discovered how delicious it is, we can't get through a bowl of cereal or a cup of coffee without it.

## PEER PRESSURE

My daughter discovered sugar when she started school. She cried "All the other kids have candy, so why can't I?" So I gave in and she soon had the sugar habit and passed it on to her younger brothers. Oh well! I tried?

## JOKE OF THE DAY

THE WORST VICE IS ADVICE

CHAPTER EIGHT

# FAMILY AFFAIRS

## DENNIS JR. DENNIS SR., JOANNE, MIKE

The four people above are my Nephew and his family.

They run a great carnival. I should know because I was a part of it for 10 years after I retired from Northwestern Bell Telephone Co. in Omaha Nebraska.

His mother Louise and Step Father Roy Harvey started it, Dennis Lynch bought it from them and his 2 boys will inherit it from him.

AND ON SHE GOES!!

# DERRICK AND ZACHARY

## GREAT GRAND KIDS

They are my pride and joy. Both are good looking, hard workers, smart, and best of all they are musical. The musical genes certainly hit them hard.

In the beginning I knew they were special, but I didn't know how special they were. I know that I sound like a Great Grandmother, but what I tell you about them is the "HONEST TO GOD TRUTH".

## MEDICAL PROBLEMS

They both have had their medical problems. Zachie was born with two bad diseases namely: Spinal Meningitis and Encephalitis. He was rushed to Children's Hospital in Omaha, Nebraska from Blair and spent a month their. At first they didn't know if he would make it, but he was cured and turned out to be one of their miracle babies. He is in great physical health now.

Then, when in high school, Derrick was playing football. He had a freak accident that tore up his right knee. He was a long time recuperating from that, but with good medical care and therapy he did. It still bothers him once in a while though.

They are hale and hardy now and about ready to graduate from college. They both worked two jobs while carrying a full load of classes and are putting themselves through. My goal was to live until they were through school. Since they are really close to graduation, I'm setting a new goal. I'm going to live now until I hold my great, great grandson or great, great grand daughter in my arms. Then I might set a new goal. I may live until that great, great grandson or great, great grand daughter starts to school. I'll be about 100 years old then.

## MUSICAL ACHIEVEMENTS

Let me tell you of one of their musical achievements. This Spring, just before their college went to recess, they had a musical and of course my *grand kids* were in it. We came to Nebraska from Florida early so we could attend. Both have beautiful voices so were in the chorus. Both had solo or duet parts, and they were accompanists; Zachy on the guitar and the piano, Derrick on the drums.

Zachy had written a song. another student sang it while Zachy accompanied him on the piano. I said to his father that I didn't know that Zachy played the piano. He said "he's played it just 3 months". He had learned to play the piano in 3 months. When I was a kid I took piano for a year, and the only thing I played on it was "Chopsticks"

## MORE THAN CHOCOLATE

I went to that musical to please Derrick and Zachy but I enjoyed it more than eating chocolate. No kidding, it put some of the Broadway Shows I've seen to shame.

Although my great grandson's names are Adkins, they come from a long, long line of singers. MOVE OVER BATHURST'S SINGERS, MAKE WAY FOR THE ADKINS BROTHERS.

## JOKE OF THE DAY

I'll get nicer if you get smarter.

# THE CARNIVAL

## A GOOD BUSNESS

Farmers, teachers, and financers have their families follow in their footsteps and form a dynasty. I know such a man, Dennis Lynch, who happens to be my nephew, has built such a dynasty in the Carnival Business. Of course his wife, Joanne, and his sons Dennis and Mike have helped him. Well, maybe it can't rightly be called a dynasty but it's a good family business.

## GRANDPA STARTED IT ALL

It all started with Dennis's Grandpa, my Dad, Roland Jay Bathurst. He was at first a teacher. Soon he discovered that teaching was too tame for his wandering soul. He had taught himself to play the guitar and violin and he had a wonderful speaking and singing voice, so he became a member of a minstrel group that performed on a Show Boat.

## STARTED HIS OWN SHOW

When he had some show business experience, he took his instruments and his voice and devised a "One Man Show" He performed in Opera Houses, School Houses and even on the street corner throughout the country. At one time his entire family, a wife Edna, and 6 kids performed with him. When we kids grew up and had left the show, he went back to his "One Man Show. After a while he found that he no longer liked traveling alone, so he joined a carnival as a "Rube" on their Midway. He also run a "Low Striker" that he built himself.

## ANNA ALOUISE

The only one of us kids who followed the carnival was my sister, Anna Louise, Dennis's mother. It was there that she met her husband and Dennis's stepfather, Roy Harvey. After a time, she and Roy formed a small carnival of their own.

## BOUGHT THE SHOW

Dennis and Joanne eventually bought the show from Roy and Louise and they have been enlarging and improving it ever since. They now have 20 rides and about the same number of concessions. The concessions are mainly owned by their friends and neighbors in Chapman and some are owned by Dennis JR. Son Michael owns some of the rides. The "Ride Boys" dress neatly and, of course, cut their hair. They have a good, clean, show. They now have rides that they bought overseas. They are as follows:

## "THE SKYMASTER"

It was bought in London, England in the year 2000, and was built in the United Kingdom, and is owned by Dennis Lynch "The Elder" and his wife, Joanne.

Dennis and his wife flew to London to buy it.

## "THE TORNADO"

The Tornado was bought in the year 2007 by the Lynches in San Salvador where it was built. It is owned by Mike Lynch.

## "FREE STYLE"

Was bought in Cork Ireland in the year 2011 and was built in the Czech Republic. It is the only one of it's kind in the U.S.A. It is owned by Mike Lynch.

## REUNION

When I was growing up I can remember all of the family getting together at the carnival. Each year when it was at a central location we would call each other and say "we'll meet you there" and we did. Can you imagine having a yearly family reunion with a carnival at your disposal and free rides for the kids?

## FAVORITE MEMORIES

That is one of my favorite memories of the carnival.

My other favorite memory is when we retired from our regular jobs and worked 10 years more with the Carnival. On the Fourth of July we would get up at 6 A.M., me driving the Motor Home and my husband driving a Truck pulling our Game Traylor behind. We drove through the hills and plaines along the Niobrara River at the extreme Northwestern boarder of Nebraska on the way to a celebration at Gregory, South Dakota. We have traveled extensively in both the U.S. and abroad and never have found scenery that compared to that.

## JOKE OF THE DAY

No matter how hard you try you can't baptize a cat.

## MORE OF ROLAND J. BATHURST'S
## REPERTOIRE

### FUNNY SONGS
WHAT ARE LITTLE GIRLS MADE OUT OF
I WENT TO SLEEP IN A RIVER

### FUNNY VERSES
LEEDLE DUTCH BABY
*(BY JAMES WHITCOME RILEY)*
USE A LITTLE WORD
THE NONSENSE RHYME

\*    \*    \*

**THESE OFFERINGS ARE UNKNOWN TO ME
THEY ARE OVER 100 YEARS OLD.
THE RAVEN** *(BY EDGAR ALLEN POE)* WAS
ONE OF THE BEST RECITATION HE USED.
A COPY IS AT THE END OF THE BOOK
WITH MY DAD'S BIOGRAPHY.
I GUESSTHAT YOU CAN TELL
THAT IT IS MY FAVORITE.
I HOPE THAT IT BECOMES SOME OF
MY READERS FAVORITE TOO.

# ME MUDDER AND FADDER

We had a large but not overly extended family.

We were always taking pictures. Among dad's talents, he was a photographer. His careers spanned being a teacher, a minstrel, a One Man Show, performed in the Bathurst Chorus and was a "Rube" on a Carnival Midway.

As soon as we kids came along Mom was just a MOM. She stayed home, took care of us kids and supported Dad in 'whatever'.

# WHAT ARE LITTLEE GIRLS MADE OUT OF

What are little girls made out of
What are little girls made out of
Sugar and spice and everything nice
That's what little girls are made out of

What are little boys made out of
What are little boys made out of
Snips and snails and puppy dog tails
That's what little boys are made out of

What are little girls made out of
What are little girls made out of
Silk dresses and lace and paint on their face
That's what little girls are made out of

What are little boys made out of
What are little boys made out of
Flying their kites and having fights
That's what little boys are made out of

# I WENT TO SLEEP IN A RIVER

I WAS BORN IN CINNCINNATEE
DOWN IN ICELAND NEAR THE SOUTH
THAT'S THE ONLY REASON WHY
MY VOICE IS IN MY MOUTH

OH I WENT TO SLEEP IN A RIVER
JUST BECAUSE IT HAD A BED
AND I TOOK A SHEET OF WATER
FOR TO COVER UP MY HEAD

OH THE PIGS WERE MAKING PIG STYS
AND THE GRASS WAS MAKING HAY
AND THE BUMBLE BEES WERE MAKING BUMS
FOR TA RA RA BUMDIA

I SHALL NE'ER FORGET THE SCHOOL MASTER
WHO GAVE ME MANY A RAP
IF HE SHOULD TRY TO DO IT NOW
HE'D NOT BE ONTHE MAP

# LEEDLE DUTCH BABY

## BY JAMES WHITCOMB RILEY

LEEDLE Dutch baby haff come ter town!
Jabber and jump 'till der day gone down—
Jabber and sphlutter and sphlit hees jaws—
   Vot a Dutch baby dees Londsmon vas!
   I dink dose mout' vas leedle too vide
     Ober he laugh fon dot also-side!
Haff got blenty off deemple und vrown?—
   Hey! leedle Dutchman come ter town!

   Leetle Dutch baby I dink me proud
   Ober your fader can schquall dot loud
   Ven he vas leetle Dutch baby like you
Und yoost don't gare, like he always do!—
Guess when dey vean him on beer, you bet,
Dots der because dot he aind veined yet!—
   Vot you said off he dringk you down?—
   Hey! leedle Dutchman come ter town!

   Leetle Dutch baby yoost schquall away—
   Schquall fon preakfast till gisterday!
   Better you all time gry und shout
Dan shmile me vonce fon der coffin out!
   Vot I gare off you keek my nose
Downside-up mit your heels und toes—
   Downside, oder der oopside-down?—
   Hey! Leedle Dutchman come ter town!

# USE A LITTLE WORD

Dad always said "Don't use a big word when you can use a little one. However he didn't always take his own advice. One of the favorite recitations he gave was as follows:

## *BIG WORDS*

*In promulgating your esoteric cogitations,*
*Or articulating your superficial sentimentalities,*
*Amicable, philosophical or physiological observations,*

*You should always be aware of platitudness ponderocity.*
*And let your extemporaneous disc antics*
*Have a clarified conciseness, compact comprehensiveness*
*Coalescent consistency,*
*Without throtamontate or thrisonical bombast*

## *LITTLE WORDS*

*In other words:*
*Always speak plainly,*
*briefly and naturally.*
*Say what you mean.*
*Mean what you say.*
*And don't always try to use a lot of big words*

## *THE RAVEN*

*ONCE UP0N A MIDNIGHT DREARY,*
*WHILE I PONDERED, WEAK AND WEARY,*
*OVER MANY A QUAINT AND CURIUS*
*VOLUME OF FORGOTTEN LORE—*
*WHILE I NODDED, NEARLY NAPPING,*
*SUDDENLY THERE CAME A TAPPING,*
*AS OF SOME ONE GENTLY RAPPING,*
*RAPPING AT MY CHAMBER DOOR.*
*"'TIS SOME VISITOR," I MUTTERED,*
*"TAPPING AT MY CHAMBER DOOR—*
*(ONLY THIS AND NOTHING MORE.")*

*AH, DISTINCTLY I REMEMBER IT*
*WAS IN THE BLEAK DECEMBER;*
*AND EACH SEPARATE DYING EMBER*
*WROUGHT ITS GHOST UPON THE FLOOR.*
*EAGERLY I WISHED THE MORROW;—*
*VAINLY I HAD SOUGHT TO BORROW*
*FROM MY BOOKS SURCEASE OF SORROW—*
*SORROW FOR THE LOST LENORE—*
*FOR THE RARE AND RADIANT MAIDEN*
*WHOM THE ANGELS NAME LENORE—*
*(NAMELESS HERE FOR EVERMORE.)*

*AND THE SILKEN, SAD, UNCERTAIN*
*RUSTLING OF EACH PURPLE CURTAIN*
*THRILLED ME—FILLED ME WITH*
*FANTASTIC TERRORS NEVER FELT BEFORE;*
*SO THAT NOW, TO STILL THE BEATING*
*OF MY HEART, I STOOD REPEATING*
*"'TIS SOME VISITOR ENTREATING*

*ENTRANCE AT MY CHAMBOR DOOR—*
*SOME LATE VISITOR ENTREATNG*
*ENTRANCE AT MY CHAMBER DOOR;—*
*(THIS IT IS AND NOTHING MORE.")*

*PRESENTLY MY SOUL GREW STRONGER;*
*HESITATING THEN NO LONGER,*
*"SIR," SAID I "OR MADAM, TRULY*
*YOUR FORGIVENESS I IMPLORE;*
*BUT THE FACT IS I WAS NAPPING,*
*AND SO GENTLY YOU CAME RAPPING,*
*AND SO FAINTLY YOU CAME TAPPING,*
*TAPPINLG AT MY CHAMBER DOOR,*
*THAT I SCARCE WAS SURE I HEARD YOU"—*
*HERE I OPENED WIDE THE DOOR;—*
*(DARKNESS THERE AND NOTHING MORE.)*

*DEEP INTO THAT DARKNESS PEERING, LONG*
*I STOOD THERE WONDERING, FEARING,*
*DOUBTING, DREAMING DREAMS NO MORTAL*
*EVER DARED TO DREAM BEFORE;*
*BUT THE SILENCE WAS UNBROKEN,*
*AND THE STILLNESS GAVE ME TOKEN,*
*AND THE ONLY WORD THERE SPOKEN*
*WAS THE WHISPERED WORD, "LENORE!"*
*THIS I WHISPERED, AND AN ECHO*
*MURMURED BACK THE WORD "LENORE!"*
*(MERELY THIS AND NOTHING MORE.)*

*BACK INTO THE CHAMBER TURNING,*
*ALL MY SOUL WITHIN ME BURNING,*
*SOON AGAIN I HEARD A TAPPING,*
*SOMEWHAT LOUDER THAN BEFORE.*

*"SURELY," SAID I, "SURELY THAT IS*
*SOMETHING AT MY WINDOW LATTICE;*
*LET ME SEE, THEN, WHAT THE THREAT IS,*
*AND THIIS MYSTERY EXPLORE—*
*LET MY HEART BE STILL A MOMENT*
*AND THIS MYSTERY EXPLORE;—*
*"TIS THE WIND AND NOTHING MORE!"*

*OPEN HERE I FLUNG THE SHUTTER, WHEN,*
*WITH MANY A FLIRT AND FLUTTER*
*IN THERE STEPPED A STATELY RAVEN*
*OF THE SAINTLY DAYS OF YORE.*
*NOT THE LEAST OBEISANCE MADE HE;*
*NOT A MINUTE STOPPED OR STAYEDHE;*
*BUT, WITH MIEN OF LORD OR LADY,*
*PERCHED ABOVE MY CHAMBER DOOR—*
*PERCHED UPON A BUST OF PALLAS*
*JUST ABOVE MY CHAMBER DOOR—*
*(PERCHED, AND SAT, AND NOTHING MORE.)*

*THEN THIS EBONY BIRD BEGUILING*
*MY SAD FANCY INTO SMILING,*
*BY THE GRAVE AND STERN DECORUM*
*OF THE COUNTENANCE IT WORE, "THOUGH*
*THY CREST BE SHORN AND SHAVEN,*
*THOU," I SAID, "ART SURE NO CRAVEN,*
*GHASTLY GRIM AND ANCIENT RAVEN*
*WANDERING FROM THE NIGHTLY SHORE—*
*TELL ME WHAT THY LORDLY NAME IS*
*ON THE NIGHT'S PLUTONIAN SHORE!"*
*(QUOTH THE RAVEN "NEVERMORE.")*
*MUCH I MARVELLED THIS UNGAINLY*
*FOWL TO HEAR DISCOURSE SO PLAINLY,*

*THOUGH IT'S ANSWER LITTLE MEANING-*
*LITTLE RNELEVACY I BORE;*
*FOR WE CANNOT HELP AGREEING*
*THAT NO LIVING HUMAN BEING*
*EVER YET WAS BLESSED WITH SEEING*
*BIRD ABOVE HIS CHAMBER DOOR—BIRD*
*OR BEAST UPON THE SCULPTURED*
*BUST ABOVE HIS CHAMBER DOOR,*
*WITH SUCH NAME AS "NEVERMORE.")*
*BUT THE RAVEN, SITTING BOLDLY*
*ON THE PLACID BUST, SPOKE ONLY*
*THAT ONE WORD, AS IF HIS SOUL*
*IN THAT ONE WORD HE DID OUTPORE.*
*NOTHING FARTHER HE DID UTTER—*
*NOT A FEATHER THEN HE FLUTTERED—*
*TILL I SCARCELY MORE THAN MUTTERED*
*"OTHER FRIENDS HAVE FLOWN BEFORE—*
*ON THE MORROW HE WILL LEAVE ME,*
*AS MY HOPES HAVE FLOWN BEFORE."*
*(THEN THE BIRD SAID "NEVERMORE.")*

*STARTLED AT THE STILLNESS BROKEN*
*BY REPLY SO APTLY SPOKEN,*
*"DOUBTLESS," SAID I "WHAT IT UTTERS*
*IS IT'S ONLY STOCK AND STORE*
*CAUGHT FROM SOME UNHAPPY MASTER*
*WHOM UNMERCIFUL DISASTER*
*FOLLOWED FAST AND FOLLOWED FAST*
*TILL HIS SONGS ONE BURDEN BORE—*
*TILL THE DIRGES OF HIS HOPE*
*THAT MELANCHOLY BURDEN BORE*
*(OF NEVERMORE—NEVERMORE.")*

*BUT THE RAVEN STILL BEGUILING*
*ALL MY FANCY INTO SMILING,*
*STRAIGHT I WHEELED A CUSHION SEAT*
*IN FRONT OF BEAST AND BUST AND DOOR;*
*THEN UPON THE VELVET SINKING,*
*I BETOOK MYSELF TO LINKING*
*FANCY UNTO FANCY, THINKING*
*WHAT THIS OMINOUS BIRD OF YORE—*
*WHAT THIS GRIM, UNGAINLY, GASTLY,*
*GAUNT, AND OMINOUS BIRD OF YORE*
*(MEANT IN CROAKING "NEVERMORE.")*

*THIS I SAT ENGAGED IN GUESSING,*
*BUT NO SYLLABLE EXPRESSING TO THE*
*THE FOWL WHOSE FIERY EYES NOW*
*BURNED INTO MY BOSOM CORE—*
*THIS AND MORE I SAT DEVINING,*
*WITH MY HEAD AT ONCE RECLINING*
*ON THE CUSHION'S VEVET LINING*
*THAT THE LAMPLIGHT GLOATING O'ER,*
*BUT WHOSE VELVET, VIOLET LINING*
*WITH THE LAMP-LIGHT GLOATING O'ER,*
*(SHE SHALL PRESS, AH, NEVERMORE)*

*THEN, ME THOUGHT, THE AIR GREW DENSER,*
*PERFUMED FROM AN UNSEEN SENSER*
*SWUNG BY SCRAP HIM WHOSE FOOT—*
*FALLS TINKLED ON THE TUFTED FLOOR.*
*"WRETCH," I CRIED THY GOD HATH LENT THEE—*
*BY THESE ANGELS HE HATH SENT THEE*
*RESPITE—RESPITE AND REPENT THEE*
*FROM MY MEMORIES OF LENORE;*

QUAFF, OH QUAFF THIS KIND NEPENT THEE
AND FORGET THIS LOST LENORE!"
(QUOTH THE RAVEN NEVERMORE.)

"PROPHET!" SAID I, "THING OF EVIL—
PROPHET STILL, IF BIRD OR DEVIL—
WHETHER TEMPTER SENT, OR WHETHER
TEMPEST TOSSED THEE HERE ASHORE,
DESOLATE YET ALL UNDAUNTED,
ON THIS DESERT LAND ENCHANTED—
ON THIS HOME BY HORRER HAUNTED—
TELL ME TRULY, I IMPLORE—
IS THERE—IS THERE BALM IN GILEAD?—
TELL ME—TELL ME, I IMPLORE!"
(QUOTH THE RAVEN "NEVERMORE.")

"PROFIT" SAID I, "THING OF EVIL!—
PROFIT STILL, IF BIRD OR DEVIL
BY THAT HEAVEN THAT BENDS ABOVE US—
BY THAT GOD WE BOTH ADORE—
TELL THIS SOUL BY SORROW LADEN IF,
WITHIN THE DISTANT AIDENN,
IT SHALL CLASP A SAINTED MAIDEN
WHOM THE ANGELS NAME LENORE—
CLASP A RARE AND RADIANT MAIDEN
WHOM THE ANGELS NAME LENORE."
(QUOTH THE RAVEN "NEVERMORE.')

'BE THAT WORD OUR SIGN OF PARTING,
BIRD OR FIEND!" I SHRIEKED, UPSTARTING—
"GET THEE BACK INTO THE TEMPEST
AND THE NIGHT'S PLUTONIAN SHORE!
LEAVE NO BLACK PLUME AS A TOKEN

VIRGINIA BATHURST BECK

*OF THAT LIE THY SOUL HATH SPOKEN!*
*LEAVE MY LONLINESS UNBROKEN!—*
*QUIT THE BUST ABOVE MY DOOR!*
*TAKE THY BEAK FROM OUT MY HEART,*
*AND TAKE THY FORM FROM OFF MY DOOR!*
*(QUOTH THE RAVEN "NEVERMORE.")*

*AND THE RAVEN NEVER FLITTING,*
*STILL IS SITTING, STILL IS SITTING*
*ON THE PALLID BUST OF PALLAS*
*JUST ABOVE MY CHAMBER DOOR;*
*AND HIS EYES HAVE ALL THE SEEMING*
*OF A DEMON'S THAT IS DREAMING,*
*AND THE LAMP-LIGHT O'ER HIM STREAMING*
*THROWS HIS SHADOW ON THE FLOOR;*
*AND MY SOUL FROM OUT THAT SHADOW*
*THAT LIES FLOATING ON THE FLOOR*

***SHALL BE LIFTED***
***"NEVERMORE"***

# DAD'S BIOGRAPHY

TO ME DAD'S LIFE IS SO INTERTWINED
WITH EDGAR ALLEN POE'S POEM 'THE
RAVEN', THAT I DECIDED TO PUT THEM
SIDE BY SIDE IN THIS COLUMN. O.K.?
DAD WAS BORN ON A FARM IN NESS
COUNTY KANSAS IN ? 1878. HE WAS
OF 10 CHILDREN. HIS FATHER WAS
MARRIED TWICE. HIS FIRST WIFE HAD
7 CHILDREN. WHEN SHE DIED HE
REMARRIED AND HIS SECOND WIFE,
HAD 3. DAD WAS ONE OF THE 3.
WHEN HE GRADUATED FROM THE
8TH GRADE HE WENT TO NORMAL
SCHOOL AND BECAME A TEACHER.
THAT WAS ALL THAT WAS NEEDED
THEN TO TEACH
HE TAUGHT FOR QUITE A WHILE
BUT THEN TEACHING BECAME TOO
TAME FOR HIS WANDERING SOUL.
HE THEN JOINED A MINSTREL GROUP
ON A SHOWBOAT. DAD HAD A
BEAUTIFUL SINGING AND SPEAKING
VOICE. HIS MOTHER HAD TAUGHT
HIM MEMORIZATION. SO HE TOOK
HIS EXPERIENCE AS A SHOWMAN ON
THE SHOWBOAT, AND DEVISED HIS
OWN "ONE MAN SHOW."
HIS SHOW INCLUDED SONGS BOTH
FUNNY AND SERIOUS, RECITATIONS

AND INSTRAMENTAL SOLOS.
HE HAD TAUGHT HIMSELF TO
PLAY BOTH THE VIOLIN AND
THE GUITAR.

HE ADVERTISED HIS SHOW BY
WALKING THE STREETS OF A
TOWN USING A MEGAPHONE
AND GIVING OUT SHOW BILLS.

HE GAVE HIS SHOW IN SCHOOLS,
OPERA HOUSES AND AS A LAST
RESORT ON A STREET CORNERS.
SINCE ENTERTAINMENT WAS
SCARCE THEN, HE ALWAYS HAD
A FULL HOUSE.

HE MET HIS WATERLOO AT
ONAWA, IOWA WHERE HE MET
AND MARRIED THE LITTLE BLUE
EYED DAMSEL NAMED EDNA
SAMPSON, WHO WAS MY MOTHER.

HE KEPT ON WITH THE SHOW.
THEY WOULD TRAVEL FROM
TOWN TO TOWN ON A MOTOR-
CYCLE WITH A SIDE CAR. THEY
WOULD STAY IN HOTEL ROOMS
OR BOARDING HOUSES WHEN
ROOMS WERE AVAILABLE, BUT
IN A TENT WHEN THEY WERE NOT.

MOM WASN'T MUCH OF AN
ENTERTAINER, BUT SHE DID
RECITE LITTLES POEMS AND
SHE SUNG DUETS WITH DAD.
MAINLY SHE BACKED DAD UP
IN WHATEVER HE WANTED TO DO.

THEN US KIDS STARTED TO
COME AND MOM HAD TO STAY
HOME AND TAKE CARE OF US.
WE WERE SIX IN ALL, 2 BOYS
AND 4 GIRLS. I WAS SECOND
FROM THE YOUNGEST.
QUIITE A HANDFULL!
DAD KEPT HIS 'ONE MAN SHOW'
GOING UNTIL WE KIDS GREW

UP A LITTLE. THEN THE OLDER
ONES JOINED DAD AND THEY
FORMED THE BATHURST
SINCE I COULDN'T SIN
THEY DIDN'T LET ME IN.
LATER THEY LET ME DANCE
WITH THE CHORUS. I LOVED IT.

BONNIE WAS THE YOUNGEST.
SHE COULD REALLY SING.
WHEN SHE JOINED THE
CHORUS SHE STOLE THE SHOW.
THE CHORUS COULD ONLY
TRAVEL IN THE SUMMER
SINCE WE ALL ATTENDED
SCHOOL IN THE WINTER.

IT WAS HARD TO HOLD A
CHORUS TOGETHER AS
WE KIDS GREW UP,
AND DAD WAS TIRED OF
TRAVELING ALONE SO HE
JOINED A CARNIVAL AS A
"RUBE" ON THE MIDWAY.

HE FINISHED HIS WORKING
CAREER WITH THE CARNIVAL.
THEN ONE DAY QUIETLY
SLPPED AWAY

**HIS TALENT WAS ENDED
HIS GOLDEN VOICE SILENT
"FOR EVERMORE"**

IN HIS OWN WORDS

This is the Eloquent Roland Jay Bathurst

In action before an audience.

**EXERPS FROM THE RAVEN**
**by**
**EDGAR ALLEN POE**

Deep into that darkness peering, long I stood there wondering, fearing, dreaming dreams no mortal ever dared to dream before. Quote the Raven:

"N E V E R M O R E"

# AUTHOR

VIRGINIA BATHURST—BECK was born in 1923 in Sioux City, Iowa. She is now a very young 90. She and husband Dan have lived in 4 states: Iowa, Texas, Nebraska and now winters in Florida.

She wrote columns for newspapers for 6 years and wrote her first book, "Life Begins at Eighty:" when she was 88 years old. The book was written from her columns. This "Pushin' Ninety the 2nd of 8 books she intends to write if she lies that long. She plans to.

!!WISH HER

LUCK AND A LONG LIFE!!